OUR DIGITAL PLANET

Staying Safe Online

by Ben Hubbard

capstone

Edited by Nikki Potts
Designed by Sarah Bennett
Picture research by Ruth Smith
Production by Laura Manthe
Originated by Capstone Global Library Limited
Printed and bound in China
007875

Library of Congress Cataloging-in-Publication Data
Cataloging-in-Publication data is available on the Library of Congress website.
ISBN 978 1 4846 3600 8

Acknowledgements
We would like to thank the following for permission to reproduce photographs: Shutterstock: Aha-Soft, 22 (attachment), Anchiy, 15, back cover right, Andrey_Popov, 13, d8nn, 6, David M G, 11, Feng Yu, 16, izabell, cover, karelnoppe, 8, Kdonmuang, 12, MIKHAIL GRACHIKOV, 22 (screen name), Monkey Business Images, 10, 22 (trusted adult), back cover left, Nadezhda1906, 9, Nikolaeva, cover design element, interior design element, Rawpixel.com, 5, Richard Cavalleri, 14, scyther5, 22 (social media), SpeedKingz, 18, 19, Studio_G, 4, Syda Productions, 20, Tinxi, 7, Valeri Potapova, 22 (password), wavebreakmedia, 17, 21, Yuliya Evstratenko, 22 (communicate)

We would like to thank Matt Anniss for his invaluable help in the preparation of this book.

Every effort has been made to contact copyright holders of material reproduced in this book. Any omissions will be rectified in subsequent printings if notice is given to the publisher.

All the internet addresses (URLs) given in this book were valid at the time of going to press. However, due to the dynamic nature of the internet, some addresses may have changed, or sites may have changed or ceased to exist since publication. While the author and publisher regret any inconvenience this may cause readers, no responsibility for any such changes can be accepted by either the author or the publisher.

Contents

Some words are shown in bold, **like this**.
You can find them in the glossary on page 22.

What Is the Internet?

The Internet is a network of computers. It connects people using underground cables that stretch around the world.

We connect to the Internet using our tablets, smart phones, and laptops. The Internet is a great place to learn, have fun, and keep in touch with friends.

How Do People Connect Online?

People often use the Internet to visit websites and learn new things. Many also **communicate** with each other using e-mail and **social media**.

You can also play games with other people online. When you are connected to the Internet you are "online."

Is Being Online Fun?

Being online is like going on an adventure. It is fun and exciting.

However, you have to be prepared. Just as on a real adventure, you don't know who or what you will discover.

Who Can Help With the Internet?

When you begin using the Internet, ask a **trusted adult** to help you. She or he can set up your computer's security settings and online **passwords**.

She or he can also help you create
a **screen name**. A screen name is a
made-up name a person uses on some
social media websites.

Is Social Media Safe?

Social media is like an online club where you can chat with friends. However, you have to be careful about chatting with people you don't know.

Sometimes people pretend to be a friend when they want something from you.

Should I Share My Personal Information?

It's important to keep any personal information off the Internet. If a friend asks for your address or phone number, share that privately, on the phone or by e-mail.

You should only use your full name or share photos with people you have met in person. Ask an adult to help you with privacy settings on **social media** sites.

Should I Ever Ignore E-mails?

E-mail is a great way to keep in touch with friends and family. It's important not to open e-mails from strangers.

Sometimes these e-mails contain **attachments** called viruses. They can harm your computer. It's best to delete such e-mails or ask an adult to help decide whether to open them.

What Are Cyberbullies?

Cyberbullies are people who say nasty things. They also spread lies about others online.

It's important never to reply to a cyberbully. You should never spread their messages. Instead, show their messages to a **trusted adult** for help.

How Can I Be a Good Digital Citizen?

Being a good digital citizen means being polite online and respecting others. Remember to always report anything you think is harmful.

That will help make the Internet an exciting, fun, and safe adventure for everyone.

Glossary

 **attachment** file, such as a photo, that is sent as part of an e-mail

 **communicate** to share information, thoughts, or feelings

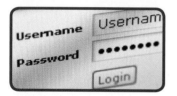 **password** secret code usually made up of a combination of letters, words, or numbers

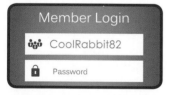 **screen name** made-up name that a person uses when he or she are online

 **social media** form of online communication where users create online communities to share information, ideas, messages, etc.

 **trusted adult** grown-up that you know well, who is honest and reliable

Find Out More

Books

McAneney, Caitlin. *Online Safety.* Let's Talk About It. New York: Powerkids Press, 2015.

Nelson, Drew. *Dealing With Cyberbullies.* Cyberspace Survival Guide. New York: Gareth Stevens Publishing, 2013.

Yearling, Tricia. *The Internet: What It Is and How to Use It.* Zoom in on Technology. New York: Enslow Publishing, 2016.

Websites

Facthound offers a safe, fun way to find Internet sites related to this book. All of the sites on Facthound have been researched by our staff.

Here's all you do:
Visit *www.facthound.com*
Type in this code: 9781484636008

Index